The Vision of the Maid of Orleans by Robert Southey

Robert Southey was born on the 12th of August 1774 in Bristol. A poet of the Romantic school and one of the "Lake Poets".

Although his fame has been eclipsed by that of his friends William Wordsworth and Samuel Taylor Coleridge, Southey's verse was highly influential and he wrote movingly against the horrors and injustice of the slave trade. Among his other classics are Inchcape Rock as well as a number of plays including Wat Tyler.

He was great friends with Coleridge, indeed in 1795, in a plan they soon abandoned, they thought to found a utopian commune-like society, called Pantisocracy, in the wilds of Pennsylvania.

However that same year, the two friends married sisters Sarah and Edith Fricker. Southey's marriage was successful but Coleridge's was not. In 1810 he abandoned his wife and three children to Southey's care in the Lake District. Although his income was small and those dependent upon him growing in number he continued to write and burnish his reputation with a wider public.

In 1813 on the refusal of Walter Scott he was offered by George II the post of Poet Laureate, a post Southey accepted and kept till his death 30 years later.

Southey was also a prolific letter writer, literary scholar, essay writer, historian and biographer. His biographies included those of John Bunyan, John Wesley, William Cowper, Oliver Cromwell and Horatio Nelson.

He was a renowned scholar of Portuguese and Spanish literature and history, and translated works from those two languages into English and wrote a History of Brazil (part of his planned but un-completed History of Portugal) and a History of the Peninsular War.

Perhaps his most enduring contribution is the children's classic The Story of the Three Bears, the original Goldilocks story, first published in Southey's prose collection The Doctor.

In 1838, Edith died and Southey married Caroline Anne Bowles, also a poet, on 4 June 1839

Robert Southey died on the 21st of March, 1843 and is buried in Crosthwaite Church in Keswick,

Index Of Contents

The First Book

Orleans was hush'd in sleep. Stretch'd on her couch
The delegated Maiden lay: with toil
Exhausted and sore anguish, soon she closed

Her heavy eye-lids; not reposing then,
For busy Phantasy, in other scenes
Awakened. Whether that superior powers,
By wise permission, prompt the midnight dream,
Instructing so the passive faculty;
Or that the soul, escaped its fleshly clog,
Flies free, and soars amid the invisible world,
And all things 'are' that 'seem'.

Along a moor,
Barren, and wide, and drear, and desolate,
She roam'd a wanderer thro' the cheerless night.
Far thro' the silence of the unbroken plain
The bittern's boom was heard, hoarse, heavy, deep,
It made most fitting music to the scene.
Black clouds, driven fast before the stormy wind,
Swept shadowing; thro' their broken folds the moon
Struggled sometimes with transitory ray,
And made the moving darkness visible.
And now arrived beside a fenny lake
She stands: amid its stagnate waters, hoarse
The long sedge rustled to the gales of night.
An age-worn bark receives the Maid, impell'd
By powers unseen; then did the moon display
Where thro' the crazy vessel's yawning side
The muddy wave oozed in: a female guides,
And spreads the sail before the wind, that moan'd
As melancholy mournful to her ear,
As ever by the dungeon'd wretch was heard
Howling at evening round the embattled towers
Of that hell-house of France, ere yet sublime
The almighty people from their tyrant's hand
Dash'd down the iron rod.

Intent the Maid
Gazed on the pilot's form, and as she gazed
Shiver'd, for wan her face was, and her eyes
Hollow, and her sunk cheeks were furrowed deep,
Channell'd by tears; a few grey locks hung down
Beneath her hood: then thro' the Maiden's veins
Chill crept the blood, for, as the night-breeze pass'd,
Lifting her tattcr'd mantle, coil'd around
She saw a serpent gnawing at her heart.

The plumeless bat with short shrill note flits by,
And the night-raven's scream came fitfully,
Borne on the hollow blast. Eager the Maid
Look'd to the shore, and now upon the bank
Leaps, joyful to escape, yet trembling still
In recollection.

There, a mouldering pile
Stretch'd its wide ruins, o'er the plain below
Casting a gloomy shade, save where the moon
Shone thro' its fretted windows: the dark Yew,
Withering with age, branched there its naked roots,
And there the melancholy Cypress rear'd
Its head; the earth was heav'd with many a mound,
And here and there a half-demolish'd tomb.

And now, amid the ruin's darkest shade,
The Virgin's eye beheld where pale blue flames
Rose wavering, now just gleaming from the earth,
And now in darkness drown'd. An aged man
Sat near, seated on what in long-past days
Had been some sculptur'd monument, now fallen
And half-obscured by moss, and gathered heaps
Of withered yew-leaves and earth-mouldering bones;
And shining in the ray was seen the track
Of slimy snail obscene. Composed his look,
His eye was large and rayless, and fix'd full
Upon the Maid; the blue flames on his face
Stream'd a pale light; his face was of the hue
Of death; his limbs were mantled in a shroud.

Then with a deep heart-terrifying voice,
Exclaim'd the Spectre, 'Welcome to these realms,
These regions of DESPAIR! O thou whose steps
By GRIEF conducted to these sad abodes
Have pierced; welcome, welcome to this gloom
Eternal, to this everlasting night,
Where never morning darts the enlivening ray,
Where never shines the sun, but all is dark,
Dark as the bosom of their gloomy King.'

So saying he arose, and by the hand
The Virgin seized with such a death-cold touch
As froze her very heart; and drawing on,
Her, to the abbey's inner ruin, led
Resistless. Thro' the broken roof the moon
Glimmer'd a scatter'd ray; the ivy twined
Round the dismantled column; imaged forms
Of Saints and warlike Chiefs, moss-canker'd now
And mutilate, lay strewn upon the ground,
With crumbled fragments, crucifixes fallen,
And rusted trophies; and amid the heap
Some monument's defaced legend spake
All human glory vain.

The loud blast roar'd
Amid the pile; and from the tower the owl
Scream'd as the tempest shook her secret nest.

He, silent, led her on, and often paus'd,
And pointed, that her eye might contemplate
At leisure the drear scene.

He dragged her on
Thro' a low iron door, down broken stairs;
Then a cold horror thro' the Maiden's frame
Crept, for she stood amid a vault, and saw,
By the sepulchral lamp's dim glaring light,
The fragments of the dead.

'Look here!' he cried,
'Damsel, look here! survey this house of Death;
O soon to tenant it! soon to increase
These trophies of mortality! for hence
Is no return. Gaze here! behold this skull,
These eyeless sockets, and these unflesh'd jaws,
That with their ghastly grinning, seem to mock
Thy perishable charms; for thus thy cheek
Must moulder. Child of Grief! shrinks not thy soul,
Viewing these horrors? trembles not thy heart
At the dread thought, that here its life's-blood soon
Now warm in life and feeling, mingle soon
With the cold clod? a thought most horrible!
So only dreadful, for reality
Is none of suffering here; here all is peace;
No nerve will throb to anguish in the grave.
Dreadful it is to think of losing life;
But having lost, knowledge of loss is not,
Therefore no ill. Haste, Maiden, to repose;
Probe deep the seat of life.'

So spake DESPAIR
The vaulted roof echoed his hollow voice,
And all again was silence. Quick her heart
Panted. He drew a dagger from his breast,
And cried again, 'Haste Damsel to repose!
One blow, and rest for ever!' On the Fiend
Dark scowl'd the Virgin with indignant eye,
And dash'd the dagger down. He next his heart
Replaced the murderous steel, and drew the Maid
Along the downward vault.

The damp earth gave
A dim sound as they pass'd: the tainted air
Was cold, and heavy with unwholesome dews.
'Behold!' the fiend exclaim'd, 'how gradual here
The fleshly burden of mortality
Moulders to clay!' then fixing his broad eye
Full on her face, he pointed where a corpse
Lay livid; she beheld with loathing look,

The spectacle abhorr'd by living man.

'Look here!' DESPAIR pursued, 'this loathsome mass
Was once as lovely, and as full of life
As, Damsel! thou art now. Those deep-sunk eyes
Once beam'd the mild light of intelligence,
And where thou seest the pamper'd flesh-worm trail,
Once the white bosom heaved. She fondly thought
That at the hallowed altar, soon the Priest
Should bless her coming union, and the torch
Its joyful lustre o'er the hall of joy,
Cast on her nuptial evening: earth to earth
That Priest consign'd her, and the funeral lamp
Glares on her cold face; for her lover went
By glory lur'd to war, and perish'd there;
Nor she endur'd to live. Ha! fades thy cheek?
Dost thou then, Maiden, tremble at the tale?
Look here! behold the youthful paramour!
The self-devoted hero!'

Fearfully
The Maid look'd down, and saw the well known face
Of THEODORE! in thoughts unspeakable,
Convulsed with horror, o'er her face she clasp'd
Her cold damp hands: 'Shrink not,' the Phantom cried,
'Gaze on! for ever gaze!' more firm he grasp'd
Her quivering arm: 'this lifeless mouldering clay,
As well thou know'st, was warm with all the glow
Of Youth and Love; this is the arm that cleaved
Salisbury's proud crest, now motionless in death,
Unable to protect the ravaged frame
From the foul Offspring of Mortality
That feed on heroes. Tho' long years were thine,
Yet never more would life reanimate
This murdered man; murdered by thee! for thou
Didst lead him to the battle from his home,
Else living there in peace to good old age:
In thy defence he died: strike deep! destroy
Remorse with Life.'

The Maid stood motionless,
And, wistless what she did, with trembling hand
Received the dagger. Starting then, she cried,
'Avaunt DESPAIR! Eternal Wisdom deals
Or peace to man, or misery, for his good
Alike design'd; and shall the Creature cry,
Why hast thou done this? and with impious pride
Destroy the life God gave?'

The Fiend rejoin'd,
'And thou dost deem it impious to destroy

The life God gave? What, Maiden, is the lot
Assigned to mortal man? born but to drag,
Thro' life's long pilgrimage, the wearying load
Of being; care corroded at the heart;
Assail'd by all the numerous train of ills
That flesh inherits; till at length worn out,
This is his consummation!--think again!
What, Maiden, canst thou hope from lengthen'd life
But lengthen'd sorrow? If protracted long,
Till on the bed of death thy feeble limbs
Outstretch their languid length, oh think what thoughts,
What agonizing woes, in that dread hour,
Assail the sinking heart! slow beats the pulse,
Dim grows the eye, and clammy drops bedew
The shuddering frame; then in its mightiest force,
Mightiest in impotence, the love of life
Seizes the throbbing heart, the faltering lips
Pour out the impious prayer, that fain would change
The unchangeable's decree, surrounding friends
Sob round the sufferer, wet his cheek with tears,
And all he loved in life embitters death!

Such, Maiden, are the pangs that wait the hour
Of calmest dissolution! yet weak man
Dares, in his timid piety, to live;
And veiling Fear in Superstition's garb,
He calls her Resignation!
Coward wretch!
Fond Coward! thus to make his Reason war
Against his Reason! Insect as he is,
This sport of Chance, this being of a day,
Whose whole existence the next cloud may blast,
Believes himself the care of heavenly powers,
That God regards Man, miserable Man,
And preaching thus of Power and Providence,
Will crush the reptile that may cross his path!

Fool that thou art! the Being that permits
Existence, 'gives' to man the worthless boon:
A goodly gift to those who, fortune-blest,
Bask in the sunshine of Prosperity,
And such do well to keep it. But to one
Sick at the heart with misery, and sore
With many a hard unmerited affliction,
It is a hair that chains to wretchedness
The slave who dares not burst it!
Thinkest thou,
The parent, if his child should unrecall'd
Return and fall upon his neck, and cry,
Oh! the wide world is comfortless, and full
Of vacant joys and heart-consuming cares,

I can be only happy in my home
With thee--my friend!--my father! Thinkest thou,
That he would thrust him as an outcast forth?
Oh I he would clasp the truant to his heart,
And love the trespass.'
Whilst he spake, his eye
Dwelt on the Maiden's cheek, and read her soul
Struggling within. In trembling doubt she stood,
Even as the wretch, whose famish'd entrails crave
Supply, before him sees the poison'd food
In greedy horror.

Yet not long the Maid
Debated, 'Cease thy dangerous sophistry,
Eloquent tempter!' cried she. 'Gloomy one!
What tho' affliction be my portion here,
Think'st thou I do not feel high thoughts of joy.
Of heart-ennobling joy, when I look back
Upon a life of duty well perform'd,
Then lift mine eyes to Heaven, and there in faith
Know my reward? I grant, were this life all,
Was there no morning to the tomb's long night,
If man did mingle with the senseless clod,
Himself as senseless, then wert thou indeed
A wise and friendly comforter! But, Fiend!
There is a morning to the tomb's long night,
A dawn of glory, a reward in Heaven,
He shall not gain who never merited.
If thou didst know the worth of one good deed
In life's last hour, thou would'st not bid me lose
The power to benefit; if I but save
A drowning fly, I shall not live in vain.
I have great duties, Fiend! me France expects,
Her heaven-doom'd Champion.'
'Maiden, thou hast done
Thy mission here,' the unbaffled Fiend replied:
'The foes are fled from Orleans: thou, perchance
Exulting in the pride of victory,
Forgettest him who perish'd! yet albeit
Thy harden'd heart forget the gallant youth;
That hour allotted canst thou not escape,
That dreadful hour, when Contumely and Shame
Shall sojourn in thy dungeon. Wretched Maid!
Destined to drain the cup of bitterness,
Even to its dregs! England's inhuman Chiefs
Shall scoff thy sorrows, black thy spotless fame,
Wit-wanton it with lewd barbarity,
And force such burning blushes to the cheek
Of Virgin modesty, that thou shalt wish
The earth might cover thee! in that last hour,
When thy bruis'd breast shall heave beneath the chains

That link thee to the stake; when o'er thy form,
Exposed unmantled, the brute multitude
Shall gaze, and thou shalt hear the ribald taunt,
More painful than the circling flames that scorch
Each quivering member; wilt thou not in vain
Then wish my friendly aid? then wish thine ear
Had drank my words of comfort? that thy hand
Had grasp'd the dagger, and in death preserved
Insulted modesty?'

Her glowing cheek
Blush'd crimson; her wide eye on vacancy
Was fix'd; her breath short panted. The cold Fiend,
Grasping her hand, exclaim'd, 'too-timid Maid,
So long repugnant to the healing aid
My friendship proffers, now shalt thou behold
The allotted length of life.'

He stamp'd the earth,
And dragging a huge coffin as his car,
Two GOULS came on, of form more fearful-foul
Than ever palsied in her wildest dream
Hag-ridden Superstition. Then DESPAIR
Seiz'd on the Maid whose curdling blood stood still.
And placed her in the seat; and on they pass'd
Adown the deep descent. A meteor light
Shot from the Daemons, as they dragg'd along
The unwelcome load, and mark'd their brethren glut
On carcasses.

Below the vault dilates
Its ample bulk. 'Look here!'--DESPAIR addrest
The shuddering Virgin, 'see the dome of DEATH!'
It was a spacious cavern, hewn amid
The entrails of the earth, as tho' to form
The grave of all mankind: no eye could reach,
Tho' gifted with the Eagle's ample ken,
Its distant bounds. There, thron'd in darkness, dwelt
The unseen POWER OF DEATH.

Here stopt the GOULS,
Reaching the destin'd spot. The Fiend leapt out,
And from the coffin, as he led the Maid,
Exclaim'd, 'Where never yet stood mortal man,
Thou standest: look around this boundless vault;
Observe the dole that Nature deals to man,
And learn to know thy friend.'
She not replied,
Observing where the Fates their several tasks
Plied ceaseless. 'Mark how short the longest web
Allowed to man! he cried; observe how soon,

Twin'd round yon never-resting wheel, they change
Their snowy hue, darkening thro' many a shade,
Till Atropos relentless shuts the sheers!'

Too true he spake, for of the countless threads,
Drawn from the heap, as white as unsunn'd snow,
Or as the lovely lilly of the vale,
Was never one beyond the little span
Of infancy untainted: few there were
But lightly tinged; more of deep crimson hue,
Or deeper sable died. Two Genii stood,
Still as the web of Being was drawn forth,
Sprinkling their powerful drops. From ebon urn,
The one unsparing dash'd the bitter wave
Of woe; and as he dash'd, his dark-brown brow
Relax'd to a hard smile. The milder form
Shed less profusely there his lesser store;
Sometimes with tears increasing the scant boon,
Mourning the lot of man; and happy he
Who on his thread those precious drops receives;
If it be happiness to have the pulse
Throb fast with pity, and in such a world
Of wretchedness, the generous heart that aches
With anguish at the sight of human woe.

To her the Fiend, well hoping now success,
'This is thy thread! observe how short the span,
And see how copious yonder Genius pours
The bitter stream of woe.' The Maiden saw
Fearless. 'Now gaze!' the tempter Fiend exclaim'd,
And placed again the poniard in her hand,
For SUPERSTITION, with sulphureal torch
Stalk'd to the loom. 'This, Damsel, is thy fate!
The hour draws on--now drench the dagger deep!
Now rush to happier worlds!'
The Maid replied,
'Or to prevent or change the will of Heaven,
Impious I strive not: be that will perform'd!'

On a rock more high
Than Nature's common surface, she beholds
The Mansion house of Fate, which thus unfolds
Its sacred mysteries. A trine within
A quadrate placed, both these encompast in
A perfect circle was its form; but what
Its matter was, for us to wonder at,
Is undiscovered left. A Tower there stands
At every angle, where Time's fatal hands
The impartial PARCAE dwell; i' the first she sees
CLOTHO the kindest of the Destinies,
From immaterial essences to cull

The seeds of life, and of them frame the wool
For LACHESIS to spin; about her flie
Myriads of souls, that yet want flesh to lie
Warm'd with their functions in, whose strength bestows
That power by which man ripe for misery grows.

Her next of objects was that glorious tower
Where that swift-fingered Nymph that spares no hour
From mortals' service, draws the various threads
Of life in several lengths; to weary beds
Of age extending some, whilst others in
Their infancy are broke: 'some blackt in sin,
Others, the favorites of Heaven, from whence
Their origin, candid with innocence;
Some purpled in afflictions, others dyed
In sanguine pleasures': some in glittering pride
Spun to adorn the earth, whilst others wear
Rags of deformity, but knots of care
No thread was wholly free from. Next to this
Fair glorious tower, was placed that black abyss
Of dreadful ATROPOS, the baleful seat
Of death and horrour, in each room repleat
With lazy damps, loud groans, and the sad sight
Of pale grim Ghosts, those terrours of the night.
To this, the last stage that the winding clew
Of Life can lead mortality unto,
FEAR was the dreadful Porter, which let in
All guests sent thither by destructive sin.

The Second Book

She spake, and lo! celestial radiance beam'd
Amid the air, such odors wafting now
As erst came blended with the evening gale,
From Eden's bowers of bliss. An angel form
Stood by the Maid; his wings, etherial white,
Flash'd like the diamond in the noon-tide sun,
Dazzling her mortal eye: all else appear'd
Her THEODORE.

Amazed she saw: the Fiend
Was fled, and on her ear the well-known voice
Sounded, tho' now more musically sweet
Than ever yet had thrill'd her charmed soul,
When eloquent Affection fondly told
The day-dreams of delight

"Beloved Maid!
Lo! I am with thee! still thy Theodore!

Hearts in the holy bands of Love combin'd,
Death has no power to sever. Thou art mine!
A little while and thou shalt dwell with me
In scenes where Sorrow is not. Cheerily
Tread thou the path that leads thee to the grave,
Rough tho' it be and painful, for the grave
Is but the threshold of Eternity.

Favour'd of Heaven! to thee is given to view
These secret realms. The bottom of the abyss
Thou treadest, Maiden! Here the dungeons are
Where bad men learn repentance; souls diseased
Must have their remedy; and where disease
Is rooted deep, the remedy is long
Perforce, and painful."

Thus the Spirit spake,
And led the Maid along a narrow path,
Dark gleaming to the light of far-off flames,
More dread than darkness. Soon the distant sound
Of clanking anvils, and the lengthened breath
Provoking fire are heard: and now they reach
A wide expanded den where all around
Tremendous furnaces, with hellish blaze,
Flamed dreadful. At the heaving bellows stood
The meagre form of Care, and as he blew
To augment the fire, the fire augmented scorch'd
His wretched limbs: sleepless for ever thus
He toil'd and toil'd, of toil to reap no end
But endless toil and never-ending woe.

An aged man went round the infernal vault,
Urging his workmen to their ceaseless task:
White were his locks, as is the wintry snow
On hoar Plinlimmon's head. A golden staff
His steps supported; powerful talisman,
Which whoso feels shall never feel again
The tear of Pity, or the throb of Love.
Touch'd but by this, the massy gates give way,
The buttress trembles, and the guarded wall,
Guarded in vain, submits. Him heathens erst
Had deified, and bowed the suppliant knee
To Plutus. Nor are now his votaries few,
Tho' he the Blessed Teacher of mankind
Hath said, that easier thro' the needle's eye
Shall the huge camel pass, than the rich man
Enter the gates of heaven. "Ye cannot serve
Your God, and worship Mammon."
"Missioned Maid!"

So spake the Angel, "know that these, whose hands

Round each white furnace ply the unceasing toil,
Were Mammon's slaves on earth. They did not spare
To wring from Poverty the hard-earn'd mite,
They robb'd the orphan's pittance, they could see
Want's asking eye unmoved; and therefore these,
Ranged round the furnace, still must persevere
In Mammon's service; scorched by these fierce fires,
And frequent deluged by the o'erboiling ore:
Yet still so framed, that oft to quench their thirst
Unquenchable, large draughts of molten gold
They drink insatiate, still with pain renewed,
Pain to destroy."

So saying, her he led
Forth from the dreadful cavern to a cell,
Brilliant with gem-born light. The rugged walls
Part gleam'd with gold, and part with silver ore
A milder radiance shone. The Carbuncle
There its strong lustre like the flamy sun
Shot forth irradiate; from the earth beneath,
And from the roof a diamond light emits;
Rubies and amethysts their glows commix'd
With the gay topaz, and the softer ray
Shot from the sapphire, and the emerald's hue,
And bright pyropus.

There on golden seats,
A numerous, sullen, melancholy train
Sat silent. "Maiden, these," said Theodore,
Are they who let the love of wealth absorb
All other passions; in their souls that vice
Struck deeply-rooted, like the poison-tree
That with its shade spreads barrenness around.
These, Maid! were men by no atrocious crime
Blacken'd, no fraud, nor ruffian violence:
Men of fair dealing, and respectable
On earth, but such as only for themselves
Heap'd up their treasures, deeming all their wealth
Their own, and given to them, by partial Heaven,
To bless them only: therefore here they sit,
Possessed of gold enough, and by no pain
Tormented, save the knowledge of the bliss
They lost, and vain repentance. Here they dwell,
Loathing these useless treasures, till the hour
Of general restitution."

Thence they past,
And now arrived at such a gorgeous dome,
As even the pomp of Eastern opulence
Could never equal: wandered thro' its halls
A numerous train; some with the red-swoln eye

Of riot, and intemperance-bloated cheek;
Some pale and nerveless, and with feeble step,
And eyes lack-lustre.

Maiden? said her guide,
These are the wretched slaves of Appetite,
Curst with their wish enjoyed. The epicure
Here pampers his foul frame, till the pall'd sense
Loaths at the banquet; the voluptuous here
Plunge in the tempting torrent of delight,
And sink in misery. All they wish'd on earth,
Possessing here, whom have they to accuse,
But their own folly, for the lot they chose?
Yet, for that these injured themselves alone,
They to the house of PENITENCE may hie,
And, by a long and painful regimen,
To wearied Nature her exhausted powers
Restore, till they shall learn to form the wish
Of wisdom, and ALMIGHTY GOODNESS grants
That prize to him who seeks it."

Whilst he spake,
The board is spread. With bloated paunch, and eye
Fat swoln, and legs whose monstrous size disgraced
The human form divine, their caterer,
Hight GLUTTONY, set forth the smoking feast.
And by his side came on a brother form,
With fiery cheek of purple hue, and red
And scurfy-white, mix'd motley; his gross bulk,
Like some huge hogshead shapen'd, as applied.
Him had antiquity with mystic rites
Ador'd, to him the sons of Greece, and thine
Imperial Rome, on many an altar pour'd
The victim blood, with godlike titles graced,
BACCHUS, or DIONUSUS; son of JOVE,
Deem'd falsely, for from FOLLY'S ideot form
He sprung, what time MADNESS, with furious hand,
Seiz'd on the laughing female. At one birth
She brought the brethren, menial here, above
Reigning with sway supreme, and oft they hold
High revels: mid the Monastery's gloom,
The sacrifice is spread, when the grave voice
Episcopal, proclaims approaching day
Of visitation, or Churchwardens meet
To save the wretched many from the gripe
Of eager Poverty, or mid thy halls
Of London, mighty Mayor! rich Aldermen,
Of coming feast hold converse.

Otherwhere,
For tho' allied in nature as in blood,

They hold divided sway, his brother lifts
His spungy sceptre. In the noble domes
Of Princes, and state-wearied Ministers,
Maddening he reigns; and when the affrighted mind
Casts o'er a long career of guilt and blood
Its eye reluctant, then his aid is sought
To lull the worm of Conscience to repose.
He too the halls of country Squires frequents,
But chiefly loves the learned gloom that shades
Thy offspring Rhedycina! and thy walls,
Granta! nightly libations there to him
Profuse are pour'd, till from the dizzy brain
Triangles, Circles, Parallelograms,
Moods, Tenses, Dialects, and Demigods,
And Logic and Theology are swept
By the red deluge.

Unmolested there
He reigns; till comes at length the general feast,
Septennial sacrifice; then when the sons
Of England meet, with watchful care to chuse
Their delegates, wise, independent men,
Unbribing and unbrib'd, and cull'd to guard
Their rights and charters from the encroaching grasp
Of greedy Power: then all the joyful land
Join in his sacrifices, so inspir'd
To make the important choice.

The observing Maid
Address'd her guide, "These Theodore, thou sayest
Are men, who pampering their foul appetites,
Injured themselves alone. But where are they,
The worst of villains, viper-like, who coil
Around the guileless female, so to sting
The heart that loves them?"
"Them," the spirit replied,
A long and dreadful punishment awaits.
For when the prey of want and infamy,
Lower and lower still the victim sinks,
Even to the depth of shame, not one lewd word,
One impious imprecation from her lips
Escapes, nay not a thought of evil lurks
In the polluted mind, that does not plead
Before the throne of Justice, thunder-tongued
Against the foul Seducer."

Now they reach'd
The house of PENITENCE. CREDULITY
Stood at the gate, stretching her eager head
As tho' to listen; on her vacant face,
A smile that promis'd premature assent;

Tho' her REGRET behind, a meagre Fiend,
Disciplin'd sorely.

Here they entered in,
And now arrived where, as in study tranced,
She sat, the Mistress of the Dome. Her face
Spake that composed severity, that knows
No angry impulse, no weak tenderness,
Resolved and calm. Before her lay that Book
That hath the words of Life; and as she read,
Sometimes a tear would trickle down her cheek,
Tho' heavenly joy beam'd in her eye the while.

Leaving her undisturb'd, to the first ward
Of this great Lazar-house, the Angel led
The favour'd Maid of Orleans. Kneeling down
On the hard stone that their bare knees had worn,
In sackcloth robed, a numerous train appear'd:
Hard-featured some, and some demurely grave;
Yet such expression stealing from the eye,
As tho', that only naked, all the rest
Was one close fitting mask. A scoffing Fiend,
For Fiend he was, tho' wisely serving here
Mock'd at his patients, and did often pour
Ashes upon them, and then bid them say
Their prayers aloud, and then he louder laughed:
For these were Hypocrites, on earth revered
As holy ones, who did in public tell
Their beads, and make long prayers, and cross themselves,
And call themselves most miserable sinners,
That so they might be deem'd most pious saints;
And go all filth, and never let a smile
Bend their stern muscles, gloomy, sullen men,
Barren of all affection, and all this
To please their God, forsooth! and therefore SCORN
Grinn'd at his patients, making them repeat
Their solemn farce, with keenest raillery
Tormenting; but if earnest in their prayer,
They pour'd the silent sorrows of the soul
To Heaven, then did they not regard his mocks
Which then came painless, and HUMILITY
Soon rescued them, and led to PENITENCE,
That She might lead to Heaven.

From thence they came,
Where, in the next ward, a most wretched band
Groan'd underneath the bitter tyranny
Of a fierce Daemon. His coarse hair was red,
Pale grey his eyes, and blood-shot; and his face
Wrinkled by such a smile as Malice wears
In ecstacy. Well-pleased he went around,

Plunging his dagger in the hearts of some,
Or probing with a poison'd lance their breasts,
Or placing coals of fire within their wounds;
Or seizing some within his mighty grasp,
He fix'd them on a stake, and then drew back,
And laugh'd to see them writhe.

"These," said the Spirit,
Are taught by CRUELTY, to loath the lives
They led themselves. Here are those wicked men
Who loved to exercise their tyrant power
On speechless brutes; bad husbands undergo
A long purgation here; the traffickers
In human flesh here too are disciplined.
Till by their suffering they have equall'd all
The miseries they inflicted, all the mass
Of wretchedness caused by the wars they waged,
The towns they burnt, for they who bribe to war
Are guilty of the blood, the widows left
In want, the slave or led to suicide,
Or murdered by the foul infected air
Of his close dungeon, or more sad than all,
His virtue lost, his very soul enslaved,
And driven by woe to wickedness.

These next,
Whom thou beholdest in this dreary room,
So sullen, and with such an eye of hate
Each on the other scowling, these have been
False friends. Tormented by their own dark thoughts
Here they dwell: in the hollow of their hearts
There is a worm that feeds, and tho' thou seest
That skilful leech who willingly would heal
The ill they suffer, judging of all else
By their own evil standard, they suspect
The aid be vainly proffers, lengthening thus
By vice its punishment."

"But who are these,"
The Maid exclaim'd, "that robed in flowing lawn,
And mitred, or in scarlet, and in caps
Like Cardinals, I see in every ward,
Performing menial service at the beck
Of all who bid them?"

Theodore replied,
These men are they who in the name of CHRIST
Did heap up wealth, and arrogating power,
Did make men bow the knee, and call themselves
Most Reverend Graces and Right Reverend Lords.
They dwelt in palaces, in purple clothed,

And in fine linen: therefore are they here;
And tho' they would not minister on earth,
Here penanced they perforce must minister:
For he, the lowly man of Nazareth,
Hath said, his kingdom is not of the world."
So Saying on they past, and now arrived
Where such a hideous ghastly groupe abode,
That the Maid gazed with half-averting eye,
And shudder'd: each one was a loathly corpse,
The worm did banquet on his putrid prey,
Yet had they life and feeling exquisite
Tho' motionless and mute.

"Most wretched men
Are these, the angel cried. These, JOAN, are bards,
Whose loose lascivious lays perpetuate
Who sat them down, deliberately lewd,
So to awake and pamper lust in minds
Unborn; and therefore foul of body now
As then they were of soul, they here abide
Long as the evil works they left on earth
Shall live to taint mankind. A dreadful doom!
Yet amply merited by that bad man
Who prostitutes the sacred gift of song!"
And now they reached a huge and massy pile,
Massy it seem'd, and yet in every blast
As to its ruin shook. There, porter fit,
REMORSE for ever his sad vigils kept.
Pale, hollow-eyed, emaciate, sleepless wretch.
Inly he groan'd, or, starting, wildly shriek'd,
Aye as the fabric tottering from its base,
Threatened its fall, and so expectant still
Lived in the dread of danger still delayed.

They enter'd there a large and lofty dome,
O'er whose black marble sides a dim drear light
Struggled with darkness from the unfrequent lamp.
Enthroned around, the MURDERERS OF MANKIND,
Monarchs, the great! the glorious! the august!
Each bearing on his brow a crown of fire,
Sat stern and silent. Nimrod he was there,
First King the mighty hunter; and that Chief
Who did belie his mother's fame, that so
He might be called young Ammon. In this court
Caesar was crown'd, accurst liberticide;
And he who murdered Tully, that cold villain,
Octavius, tho' the courtly minion's lyre
Hath hymn'd his praise, tho' Maro sung to him,
And when Death levelled to original clay
The royal carcase, FLATTERY, fawning low,
Fell at his feet, and worshipped the new God.

Titus was here, the Conqueror of the Jews,
He the Delight of human-kind misnamed;
Caesars and Soldans, Emperors and Kings,
Here they were all, all who for glory fought,
Here in the COURT OF GLORY, reaping now
The meed they merited.

As gazing round
The Virgin mark'd the miserable train,
A deep and hollow voice from one went forth;
"Thou who art come to view our punishment,
Maiden of Orleans! hither turn thine eyes,
For I am he whose bloody victories
Thy power hath rendered vain. Lo! I am here,
The hero conqueror of Azincour,
HENRY OF ENGLAND!--wretched that I am,
I might have reigned in happiness and peace,
My coffers full, my subjects undisturb'd,
And PLENTY and PROSPERITY had loved
To dwell amongst them: but mine eye beheld
The realm of France, by faction tempest-torn,
And therefore I did think that it would fall
An easy prey. I persecuted those
Who taught new doctrines, tho' they taught the truth:
And when I heard of thousands by the sword
Cut off, or blasted by the pestilence,
I calmly counted up my proper gains,
And sent new herds to slaughter. Temperate
Myself, no blood that mutinied, no vice
Tainting my private life, I sent abroad
MURDER and RAPE; and therefore am I doom'd,
Like these imperial Sufferers, crown'd with fire,
Here to remain, till Man's awaken'd eye
Shall see the genuine blackness of our deeds,
And warn'd by them, till the whole human race,
Equalling in bliss the aggregate we caus'd
Of wretchedness, shall form ONE BROTHERHOOD,
ONE UNIVERSAL FAMILY OF LOVE."

Ay, you are wretched, miserably wretched,
Almost condemn'd alive! There is a place,
(List daughter!) in a black and hollow vault,
Where day is never seen; there shines no sun,
But flaming horror of consuming fires;
A lightless sulphur, choak'd with smoaky foggs
Of an infected darkness. In this place
Dwell many thousand thousand sundry sorts
Of never-dying deaths; there damned souls
Roar without pity, there are gluttons fed
With toads and adders; there is burning oil
Pour'd down the drunkard's throat, 'the usurer

Is forced to sup whole draughts of molten gold';
There is the murderer for ever stabb'd,
Yet can he never die; there lies the wanton
On racks of burning steel, whilst in his soul
He feels the torment of his raging lust.

The Third Book

The Maiden, musing on the Warrior's words,
Turn'd from the Hall of Glory. Now they reach'd
A cavern, at whose mouth a Genius stood,
In front a beardless youth, whose smiling eye
Beam'd promise, but behind, withered and old,
And all unlovely. Underneath his feet
Lay records trampled, and the laurel wreath
Now rent and faded: in his hand he held
An hour-glass, and as fall the restless sands,
So pass the lives of men. By him they past
Along the darksome cave, and reach'd a stream,
Still rolling onward its perpetual waves,
Noiseless and undisturbed. Here they ascend
A Bark unpiloted, that down the flood,
Borne by the current, rush'd. The circling stream,
Returning to itself, an island form'd;
Nor had the Maiden's footsteps ever reach'd
The insulated coast, eternally
Rapt round the endless course; but Theodore
Drove with an angel's will the obedient bark.

They land, a mighty fabric meets their eyes,
Seen by its gem-born light. Of adamant
The pile was framed, for ever to abide
Firm in eternal strength. Before the gate
Stood eager EXPECTATION, as to list
The half-heard murmurs issuing from within,
Her mouth half-open'd, and her head stretch'd forth.
On the other side there stood an aged Crone,
Listening to every breath of air; she knew
Vague suppositions and uncertain dreams,
Of what was soon to come, for she would mark
The paley glow-worm's self-created light,
And argue thence of kingdoms overthrown,
And desolated nations; ever fill'd
With undetermin'd terror, as she heard
Or distant screech-owl, or the regular beat
Of evening death-watch.

"Maid," the Spirit cried,
Here, robed in shadows, dwells FUTURITY.

There is no eye hath seen her secret form,
For round the MOTHER OF TIME, unpierced mists
Aye hover. Would'st thou read the book of Fate,
Enter."

The Damsel for a moment paus'd,
Then to the Angel spake: "All-gracious Heaven!
Benignant in withholding, hath denied
To man that knowledge. I, in faith assured,
That he, my heavenly Father, for the best
Ordaineth all things, in that faith remain
Contented."

"Well and wisely hast thou said,
So Theodore replied; "and now O Maid!
Is there amid this boundless universe
One whom thy soul would visit? is there place
To memory dear, or visioned out by hope,
Where thou would'st now be present? form the wish,
And I am with thee, there."

His closing speech
Yet sounded on her ear, and lo! they stood
Swift as the sudden thought that guided them,
Within the little cottage that she loved.
"He sleeps! the good man sleeps!" enrapt she cried,
As bending o'er her Uncle's lowly bed
Her eye retraced his features. "See the beads
That never morn nor night he fails to tell,
Remembering me, his child, in every prayer.
Oh! quiet be thy sleep, thou dear old man!
Good Angels guard thy rest! and when thine hour
Is come, as gently mayest thou wake to life,
As when thro' yonder lattice the next sun
Shall bid thee to thy morning orisons!
Thy voice is heard, the Angel guide rejoin'd,
He sees thee in his dreams, he hears thee breathe
Blessings, and pleasant is the good man's rest.
Thy fame has reached him, for who has not heard
Thy wonderous exploits? and his aged heart
Hath felt the deepest joy that ever yet
Made his glad blood flow fast. Sleep on old Claude!
Peaceful, pure Spirit, be thy sojourn here,
And short and soon thy passage to that world
Where friends shall part no more!

"Does thy soul own
No other wish? or sleeps poor Madelon
Forgotten in her grave? seest thou yon star,"
The Spirit pursued, regardless of her eye
That look'd reproach; "seest thou that evening star

Whose lovely light so often we beheld
From yonder woodbine porch? how have we gazed
Into the dark deep sky, till the baffled soul,
Lost in the infinite, returned, and felt
The burthen of her bodily load, and yearned
For freedom! Maid, in yonder evening slar
Lives thy departed friend. I read that glance,
And we are there!"

He said and they had past
The immeasurable space.
Then on her ear
The lonely song of adoration rose,
Sweet as the cloister'd virgins vesper hymn,
Whose spirit, happily dead to earthly hopes
Already lives in Heaven. Abrupt the song
Ceas'd, tremulous and quick a cry
Of joyful wonder rous'd the astonish'd Maid,
And instant Madelon was in her arms;
No airy form, no unsubstantial shape,
She felt her friend, she prest her to her heart,
Their tears of rapture mingled.

She drew back
And eagerly she gazed on Madelon,
Then fell upon her neck again and wept.
No more she saw the long-drawn lines of grief,
The emaciate form, the hue of sickliness,
The languid eye: youth's loveliest freshness now
Mantled her cheek, whose every lineament
Bespake the soul at rest, a holy calm,
A deep and full tranquillity of bliss.

"Thou then art come, my first and dearest friend!"
The well known voice of Madelon began,
"Thou then art come! and was thy pilgrimage
So short on earth? and was it painful too,
Painful and short as mine? but blessed they
Who from the crimes and miseries of the world
Early escape!"

"Nay," Theodore replied,
She hath not yet fulfill'd her mortal work.
Permitted visitant from earth she comes
To see the seat of rest, and oftentimes
In sorrow shall her soul remember this,
And patient of the transitory woe
Partake the anticipated peace again."
"Soon be that work perform'd!" the Maid exclaimed,
"O Madelon! O Theodore! my soul,
Spurning the cold communion of the world,

Will dwell with you! but I shall patiently,
Yea even with joy, endure the allotted ills
Of which the memory in this better state
Shall heighten bliss. That hour of agony,
When, Madelon, I felt thy dying grasp,
And from thy forehead wiped the dews of death,
The very horrors of that hour assume
A shape that now delights."

"O earliest friend!
I too remember," Madelon replied,
"That hour, thy looks of watchful agony,
The suppressed grief that struggled in thine eye
Endearing love's last kindness. Thou didst know
With what a deep and melancholy joy
I felt the hour draw on: but who can speak
The unutterable transport, when mine eyes,
As from a long and dreary dream, unclosed
Amid this peaceful vale, unclos'd on him,
My Arnaud! he had built me up a bower,
A bower of rest.--See, Maiden, where he comes,
His manly lineaments, his beaming eye
The same, but now a holier innocence
Sits on his cheek, and loftier thoughts illume
The enlighten'd glance."

They met, what joy was theirs
He best can feel, who for a dear friend dead
Has wet the midnight pillow with his tears.

Fair was the scene around; an ample vale
Whose mountain circle at the distant verge
Lay softened on the sight; the near ascent
Rose bolder up, in part abrupt and bare,
Part with the ancient majesty of woods
Adorn'd, or lifting high its rocks sublime.
The river's liquid radiance roll'd beneath,
Beside the bower of Madelon it wound
A broken stream, whose shallows, tho' the waves
Roll'd on their way with rapid melody,
A child might tread. Behind, an orange grove
Its gay green foliage starr'd with golden fruit;
But with what odours did their blossoms load
The passing gale of eve! less thrilling sweet
Rose from the marble's perforated floor,
Where kneeling at her prayers, the Moorish queen
Inhaled the cool delight, and whilst she asked
The Prophet for his promised paradise,
Shaped from the present scene its utmost joys.
A goodly scene! fair as that faery land
Where Arthur lives, by ministering spirits borne

From Camlan's bloody banks; or as the groves
Of earliest Eden, where, so legends say,
Enoch abides, and he who rapt away
By fiery steeds, and chariotted in fire,
Past in his mortal form the eternal ways;
And John, beloved of Christ, enjoying there
The beatific vision, sometimes seen
The distant dawning of eternal day,
Till all things be fulfilled.

"Survey this scene!"
So Theodore address'd the Maid of Arc,
"There is no evil here, no wretchedness,
It is the Heaven of those who nurst on earth
Their nature's gentlest feelings. Yet not here
Centering their joys, but with a patient hope,
Waiting the allotted hour when capable
Of loftier callings, to a better state
They pass; and hither from that better state
Frequent they come, preserving so those ties
That thro' the infinite progressiveness
Complete our perfect bliss.

"Even such, so blest,
Save that the memory of no sorrows past
Heightened the present joy, our world was once,
In the first aera of its innocence
Ere man had learnt to bow the knee to man.
Was there a youth whom warm affection fill'd,
He spake his honest heart; the earliest fruits
His toil produced, the sweetest flowers that deck'd
The sunny bank, he gather'd for the maid,
Nor she disdain'd the gift; for VICE not yet
Had burst the dungeons of her hell, and rear'd
Those artificial boundaries that divide
Man from his species. State of blessedness!
Till that ill-omen'd hour when Cain's stern son
Delved in the bowels of the earth for gold,
Accursed bane of virtue! of such force
As poets feign dwelt in the Gorgon's locks,
Which whoso saw, felt instant the life-blood
Cold curdle in his veins, the creeping flesh
Grew stiff with horror, and the heart forgot
To beat. Accursed hour! for man no more
To JUSTICE paid his homage, but forsook
Her altars, and bow'd down before the shrine
Of WEALTH and POWER, the Idols he had made.
Then HELL enlarged herself, her gates flew wide,
Her legion fiends rush'd forth. OPPRESSION came
Whose frown is desolation, and whose breath
Blasts like the Pestilence; and POVERTY,

A meagre monster, who with withering touch
Makes barren all the better part of man,
MOTHER OF MISERIES. Then the goodly earth
Which God had fram'd for happiness, became
One theatre of woe, and all that God
Had given to bless free men, these tyrant fiends
His bitterest curses made. Yet for the best
Hath he ordained all things, the ALL-WISE!
For by experience rous'd shall man at length
Dash down his Moloch-Idols, Samson-like
And burst his fetters, only strong whilst strong
Believed. Then in the bottomless abyss
OPPRESSION shall be chain'd, and POVERTY
Die, and with her, her brood of Miseries;
And VIRTUE and EQUALITY preserve
The reign of LOVE, and Earth shall once again
Be Paradise, whilst WISDOM shall secure
The state of bliss which IGNORANCE betrayed."

"Oh age of happiness!" the Maid exclaim'd,
Roll fast thy current, Time till that blest age
Arrive! and happy thou my Theodore,
Permitted thus to see the sacred depths
Of wisdom!"

"Such," the blessed Spirit replied,
Beloved! such our lot; allowed to range
The vast infinity, progressive still
In knowledge and encreasing blessedness,
This our united portion. Thou hast yet
A little while to sojourn amongst men:
I will be with thee! there shall not a breeze
Wanton around thy temples, on whose wing
I will not hover near! and at that hour
When from its fleshly sepulchre let loose,
Thy phoenix soul shall soar, O best-beloved!
I will be with thee in thine agonies,
And welcome thee to life and happiness,
Eternal infinite beatitude!"

He spake, and led her near a straw-roof'd cot,
LOVE'S Palace. By the Virtues circled there,
The cherub listen'd to such melodies,
As aye, when one good deed is register'd
Above, re-echo in the halls of Heaven.
LABOUR was there, his crisp locks floating loose,
Clear was his cheek, and beaming his full eye,
And strong his arm robust; the wood nymph HEALTH
Still follow'd on his path, and where he trod
Fresh flowers and fruits arose. And there was HOPE,
The general friend; and PITY, whose mild eye

Wept o'er the widowed dove; and, loveliest form,
Majestic CHASTITY, whose sober smile
Delights and awes the soul; a laurel wreath
Restrain'd her tresses, and upon her breast
The snow-drop hung its head, that seem'd to grow
Spontaneous, cold and fair: still by the maid
LOVE went submiss, wilh eye more dangerous
Than fancied basilisk to wound whoe'er
Too bold approached; yet anxious would he read
Her every rising wish, then only pleased
When pleasing. Hymning him the song was rais'd.

"Glory to thee whose vivifying power
Pervades all Nature's universal frame!
Glory to thee CREATOR LOVE! to thee,
Parent of all the smiling CHARITIES,
That strew the thorny path of Life with flowers!
Glory to thee PRESERVER! to thy praise
The awakened woodlands echo all the day
Their living melody; and warbling forth
To thee her twilight song, the Nightingale
Holds the lone Traveller from his way, or charms
The listening Poet's ear. Where LOVE shall deign
To fix his seat, there blameless PLEASURE sheds
Her roseate dews; CONTENT will sojourn there,
And HAPPINESS behold AFFECTION'S eye
Gleam with the Mother's smile. Thrice happy he
Who feels thy holy power! he shall not drag,
Forlorn and friendless, along Life's long path
To Age's drear abode; he shall not waste
The bitter evening of his days unsooth'd;
But HOPE shall cheer his hours of Solitude,
And VICE shall vainly strive to wound his breast,
That bears that talisman; and when he meets
The eloquent eye of TENDERNESS, and hears
The bosom-thrilling music of her voice;
The joy he feels shall purify his Soul,
And imp it for anticipated Heaven."

Robert Southey – A Concise Bibliography

The Fall of Robespierre (1794)
Joan of Arc (1796)
Icelandic Poetry, or The Edda of Sæmund (1797)
Poems (1797–1799)
Letters Written During a Short Residence in Spain and Portugal (1797)
St. Patrick's Purgatory (1798)
After Blenheim (1798)
The Devil's Thoughts (1799). Revised edition published in 1827 as "The Devil's Walk".

English Eclogues (1799)
The Old Man's Comforts and How He Gained Them (1799)
Thalaba the Destroyer (1801)
The Inchcape Rock (1802)
Madoc (1805)
Letters from England: By Don Manuel Alvarez Espriella (1807), the observations of a fictitious
Spaniard.
Chronicle of the Cid. Translated from the Spanish (1808)
The Curse of Kehama (1810)
History of Brazil (3 volumes) (1810–1819)
The Life of Horatio, Lord Viscount Nelson (1813)
Roderick the Last of the Goths (1814)
Sir Thomas Malory's Le Morte D'Arthur (1817)
Wat Tyler: A Dramatic Poem (1817)
Cataract of Lodore (1820)
The Life of Wesley; and Rise and Progress of Methodism (2 volumes) (1820)
What Are Little Boys Made Of? (1820)
The Vision of Judgement (1821)
History of the Peninsular War, 1807-1814 (3 volumes) (1823-1832)
Sir Thomas More; or, Colloquies on the Progress and Prospects of Society (1829)
The Works of William Cowper (15 vols.) (Editor) (1833-1837)
Lives of the British Admirals, with an Introductory View of the Naval History of England (5 volumes)
(1833-40); republished as "English Seamen" in 1895.
The Doctor (7 volumes) (1834-1847). Includes The Story of the Three Bears (1837).
The Poetical Works of Robert Southey, Collected by Himself (1837)